NIC BISHOP
LIZARDS

Written and
photographed by
Nic Bishop

Scholastic Inc.

Lizards are *reptiles*, like snakes, crocodiles, and turtles. They have tough, scaly, waterproof skin, which protects their bodies and stops them from drying out.

Some lizards live in sand dunes. This sandfish swims beneath the desert by wriggling its body like a little shark.

Others climb trees. Chameleons have special feet that look like mittens and clamp tight to branches.

A few lizards even glide through the air. This flying dragon opens flaps of skin like wings as it sails from tree to tree.

Most lizards hatch from eggs,
which are hidden underground,

beneath a log, or even in a
termite nest.

The babies look like their parents. This bearded dragon has legs for running, claws for gripping, and a tail for balance. And it is ready to find food.

Some lizards eat plants, but most hunt for *prey*.

A chameleon will wait for prey to come close. Then it snaps the prey up with its long, sticky tongue.

The thorny devil laps up ants, one by one. It can eat a thousand in one meal!

Komodo dragons are big enough to eat pigs, goats, and even water buffalo. They have large teeth and *venom* to overpower their prey.

But lizards
must also
watch out
for *predators*.

This gecko
hides by
looking like
an old leaf.

The frilled dragon tries to scare enemies away. It has a large ruffle of skin around its head that opens like an umbrella.

A basilisk will flee across water.
It sprints so fast that its feet barely
have time to sink.

If a lizard stays safe, it may live for five to ten years, or even longer.

A lizard may lay dozens of eggs
during its life, which hatch into
more baby lizards.

A Closer Look
with Nic Bishop

Lizards were around more than 150 million years ago, at the time of the dinosaurs. Some probably stole dinosaur eggs for food. Today, there are about 5,000 types of lizards. They come in more shapes and sizes than you might imagine. The smallest, a dwarf gecko, is so tiny that it can get caught in a spiderweb. The Komodo dragon is the world's largest lizard. It can grow ten feet long, and it has teeth almost an inch in size.

I had many adventures while taking the pictures for this book. I traveled to the remote deserts of Australia to find the thorny devil. I stayed up all night waiting for bearded dragon eggs to hatch so I could photograph them the moment they appeared. I even built a pond inside my house to take photographs of the basilisk running across the surface of the water. It was an amazing sight!

Glossary

predators: animals that live by hunting other animals for food

prey: animals that are hunted by another animal for food

reptiles: a class of animals that includes lizards, snakes, turtles, tuatara, and alligators and crocodiles

venom: a poison that passes into a victim's body through a bite or sting

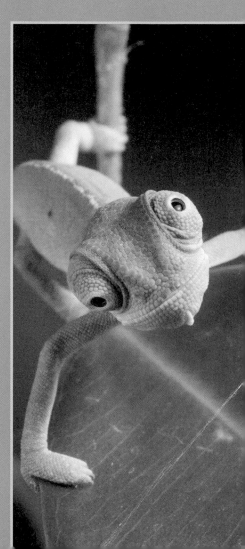

Photo Index

knob-tailed gecko,
page 1

crocodile skink,
pages 2–3

sandfish,
page 4

Jackson's chameleon,
page 5, back cover

flying dragon,
pages 6–7, 32

bearded dragon,
pages 8–9, 10–11, 26, 27, 28

leaf-tailed gecko,
pages 12, 20–21

veiled chameleon,
pages 14–15, 29, front cover

thorny devil,
pages 16–17

Komodo dragon,
pages 18–19

frilled dragon,
page 23

basilisk,
pages 24–25

ISBN 978-0-545-60569-4

Copyright © 2014 by Nic Bishop

All rights reserved. Published by Scholastic Inc. SCHOLASTIC and associated logos are trademarks and/or registered trademarks of Scholastic Inc.

12 11 10 9 8 7 6 5 4 3 2 1   14 15 16 17 18 19/0

Printed in the U.S.A. 40
First printing, January 2014